WATER MUSIC
and
MUSIC FOR THE ROYAL FIREWORKS
in Full Score

George Frideric Handel

WATER MUSIC
and
MUSIC FOR THE ROYAL FIREWORKS
in Full Score

From the Deutsche Händelgesellschaft Edition

Edited by
FRIEDRICH CHRYSANDER

Dover Publications, Inc., New York

Published in Canada by General Publishing Company, Ltd., 30 Lesmill Road,
Don Mills, Toronto, Ontario.
Published in the United Kingdom by Constable and Company, Ltd.

This Dover edition, first published in 1986, contains, unabridged and unaltered,
the works "Water Music" and "Music for the Royal Fireworks" from Volume 47 of
Georg Friedrich Händel's Werke as originally published by the Deutsche Händelgesellschaft in Leipzig in 1886.
The publisher is grateful to the Paul Klapper Library of Queens College for
making its material available for reproduction.

Manufactured in the United States of America
Dover Publications, Inc., 31 East 2nd Street, Mineola, N.Y. 11501

Library of Congress Cataloging-in-Publication Data

Handel, George Frideric, 1685–1759.
  [Water music]
  Water music ; and, Music for the royal fireworks.

  Suites, for orchestra.
  Reprint. Originally published: Leipzig : Deutsche Händelgesellschaft, 1886.
(George Friedrich Händel's Werke ; v. 47)
    1. Suites (Orchestra)—Scores. I. Chrysander, Friedrich, 1826–1901.
II. Handel, George Frideric, 1685–1759. Music for the royal fireworks.
1986. III. Water music. IV. Music for the royal fireworks.
M1003.H135W43 1986   85-754880
ISBN 0-486-25070-9

CONTENTS

WATER MUSIC

OVERTURE.

Hautboy solo.

Violino I.

Violino II.

Violino I ripieno.

Violino II ripieno.

Tenor.

Bassoon e
Violoncello.

Basso Continuo.

Andante.

Dal Segno.
(pag. 11.)

Da Capo.
(pag. 22.)

AIR.
3 fois.

3 fois.

Corno I.

Corno II.

Oboe I.

Oboe II.

Bassons.

Violino I.

Violino II.

Viola.

(Bassi.)

BOURRÉE.

3 times:— First all the Violins,— 2.ᵈ all the Hautboys,— 3.ᵈ all together.

(Tutti.)

(Viola.)

(Bassi.)

HORNPIPE.
3 times.

Violino I.
Oboe I.

Violino II.
Oboe II.

Viola.

(Tutti Bassi.)

Oboe I.
Oboe II.
Bassons.
Violino I.
Violino II.
Viola.
Bassi.

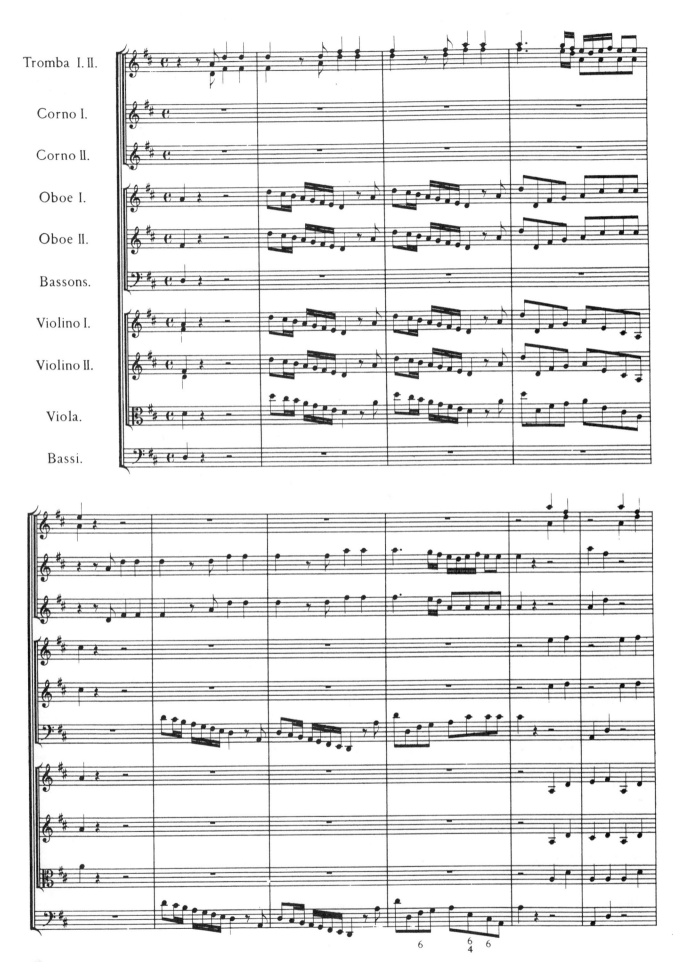

Tromba I. II.

Corno I.

Corno II.

Oboe I.

Oboe II.

Bassons.

Violino I.

Violino II.

Viola.

Bassi.

Da Capo.
(pag. 40.)

ARIA.

Da Capo.
(pag. 49.)

This Air to be played 3 times over.

MENUET.

Da Capo.
(pag. 52.)

Flauti piccoli.

Violino I.

Violino II.

Viola. Violonc.
(e Cembalo.)

CORO.

FINE.

MUSIC FOR THE ROYAL FIREWORKS

OUVERTURE.

BOURRÉE.
2 fois.

Oboe e Viol. I.
for 12.

Oboe e Viol. II.
for 12.

Bassons tutti.
(Violonc. e Contrab.)

Viola colli Bassi.

La seconda volta *senza Hautb: e Bassons.*

La Paix.

Largo alla Siciliana.

Corno I.
for **3** persons.

Corno II.
for **3** persons.

Corno III.
for **3** persons.

Oboe, Tr. e Viol. I.
for **12** persons.

Oboe. Tr. e Viol. II.
for **12** persons.

Violonc. e Contrab.;
Bassons tutti.

Viola colli Bassi.

La Rejouissance.

The second time *by the French Horns and Hautbois and Bassons without Trumpets.*
The third time *all together.*

MENUET.
2 fois.

Viol. e Oboe I.

Viol. e Oboe II.

Viola colla Bassi.

Tutti Bassi.

MENUET.

Tromba I.

Tromba II.

Principal.

Corno I. II.

Corno III.

Tympani.

Oboe I. (Violino I.)

Oboe II. (Violino II.)

(Viola.)

Tutti Bassons.

(Violoncelli, etc.)

La seconda volta

colli Corni di caccia. Hautbois et Bassons et Tympani.

La terza volta

tutti insieme, and the Side Drums.

FINE.